What Our Readers Have Said...

"Although I consider myself a seasoned sales professional, it is helpful to have past learning's refreshed. The books were also beneficial because of the information concerning 'trends' in the sales relationship. The sales process should be viewed as dynamic since business relationships change regularly."

•

"For the particular business I am in and the type of sales calls I have, I find that the books in the Pinpoint Sales Training Series are very often applicable to how I conduct business. I would recommend them to other sales people, just not ones that are in my industry."

•

"These books provide very good concepts. It fits in well with the Bell Leadership training program that I attended in November."

•

"I use this material in these books and apply it to my customers and other employees I work with."

•

"I would like to know other topics. Is there anything on Production Management or Consultative Selling or Time Management?"

•

"These books are great tools that should be used as guidelines for our everyday

supervisory practices. You need to take the time to do a short self-evaluation when reading them."

•

"The Pinpoint Training Series delivers information that could be used in a lot different areas."

•

"I like this because I can take them with me to read at a convenient time. I feel the little time I have to spend in the office is best use on activities that directly relate to revenue opportunities. I like the short amount of time it takes to keep up with these."

•

"I prefer the self-study approach; it fits in with my schedule."

•

"My thought is that the real value of these books comes into effect when doing the action plans."

•

"Short and sweet. These books are easy to comprehend."

•

"I have enjoyed reading these books. They are relevant to today's work environment and the ongoing change in the way we manage our workforce."

•

"I do feel that these books have been very helpful to me at my job."

•

"I think a lot of the recommendations in these books are very useful, and can be applicable to everyday situations. If nothing else, it's a good reference guide to fall back upon if a situation arises in the future."

•

"These books are relevant to today's work environment and the ongoing change in the way we manage our workforce."

•

Delivering Memorable Sales Presentations

Pinpoint Sales Skill Development Training Series

TIMOTHY F. BEDNARZ

MAJORIUM
BUSINESS PRESS

Pinpoint Sales Skill Development Training Series
"Delivering Memorable Sales Presentations"
Timothy F. Bednarz

Graphic design: Monika Pawlak

Majorium Business Press
2025 Main Street
Stevens Point, WI 54481
715.342.1018 • 800.654.4935

ISBN 978-1-882181-89-6

Printed in the United States of America

Introduction

The Pinpoint Sales Skill Development Training Series is designed for targeted training and education regarding increased improvement in a specific skill or competency.

Each book within this series is designed to be easy to use, understand and apply to your job. It can be used as a basis for training individuals, as a discussion guide or as a personal training tool.

Each chapter within this book discusses a specific concept. When you have completed all eight chapters you should have a 360° perspective of the topic.

Additionally, each chapter is divided into specific sections:

- The first section provides you with an overview of the topic
- The Implications section discusses why the concept is important, and why it is important to learn and apply.
- The Strategies, Tips & Techniques to Apply section teaches how to use and apply the particular concept to your work.
- The Points to Ponder section gives you something to think about or to be discussed with a group setting. These are questions not meant to be immediately answered, but to be pondered over time.
- The Training Activity section provides you with the tools to transfer what you have learned to your job. It is designed to help create an action plan to effectively apply the concept.

Each of the topics in this series is time-tested and proven in the marketplace. They have been used by thousands of employees as training tools. Many of the users have commented that what made these books valuable, was the ability to refer to them when a problem surfaced. They indicated that they remembered reading about the exact problem. They referred back to these books and found an appropriate solution.

You will find them equally valuable as a resource in your professional development library.

Table of Contents

LEARNING OBJECTIVES:

- The purpose of a sales presentation.
- The effective use and timing of a presentation.
- To prepare and use sales proposals as selling tools.
- To apply effective presentation techniques.
- To obtain results through the effective use of sales presentations.

1

The Preparation Behind a Sales Presentation

Effective sales presentations must be developed from the prospect or customer's viewpoint, and not from that of the salesperson. Salespeople must invest the time to understand and appreciate their prospect or customer's viewpoint and perspective. When the needs of the prospect or customer are considered, the presentation's focus shifts—and yields far better results.

IMPLICATIONS – WHAT THIS MEANS TO YOU

Salespeople have volumes of information and data at their disposal. Throwing everything at a prospect or customer during a presentation will lead to "information dump"—not the sale.

When salespeople understand the prospect or customer's viewpoint or perspective, they can distill their knowledge, expertise, and vast pool of information into a targeted presentation that provides the prospect or customer with the exact information and knowledge they need to make an informed decision and purchase.

This is important for salespeople to understand because most managers today are drowning in a pool of information, but starving for knowledge. Salespeople must furnish the specific knowledge their customer is looking for. In so doing they provide a genuine service by helping them make an informed purchasing decision.

STRATEGIES, TIPS & TECHNIQUES TO APPLY

Salespeople need sufficient background information regarding the prospect or customer's business before they can make a solid presentation. Without this hard information, they are literally flying blind and guessing at what the prospect or customer is interested in. This knowledge includes but is not limited to:

Company Background

The company background profile should include key information about the prospect or customer's company. Specific elements of this information include key facts about the company as they pertain to both the sale and the presentation. Few things will turn a prospect off faster than displaying ignorance of the industry in which they work.

Needs and Concerns

Through qualifying and probing, salespeople should have identified the specific needs, concerns and problems faced by the prospect or customer. This should include points of pain and discontent with the current situation. Without this information, salespeople will be unable to develop a convincing presentation.

Application

The same products and services can be used differently depending on specific applications at one or more locations. As physical environment factors can impact the performance of a product or service, salespeople should be aware of how theirs will be specifically used and in what environment. Equipped with this knowledge, salespeople can address any such potential issues and present viable solutions to overcome adverse physical environments.

Requirements

Salespeople should be aware of all specific requirements the prospect or customer may have. These include product specifications as well as anticipated volumes and ordering patterns.

Existing Solution

Unless they are facing a new opportunity within the prospect or customer's business, salespeople should be knowledgeable about the solution that is currently in place. Salespeople can use their competitive and product knowledge to craft solutions in a manner that presents their answer as superior to the existing approach causing the customer pain and discontent.

Competitive Situation

Salespeople should be aware of the competitive environment including the current vendor and other potential suppliers being considered by the prospect/customer. Only with this knowledge can salespeople use their expertise to favorably position themselves against the competition.

Who Will Attend

Salespeople should know who will be in attendance at the sales presentation—including names, titles and responsibilities—and pay special attention to the presence of key decision makers. Where possible, the presentation should be postponed until decision makers are able to attend.

'Hot-Button' Topics

Salespeople should be aware of the points that interest the prospect or customer—more commonly referred to as their "hot buttons." Individuals will only be interested in the information that addresses these issues. All other information, even if important, will be of little interest. As prospects and clients appreciate knowing their time is valued, and are irritated when it is not, salespeople must know specifically what information the customer wants and needs to hear.

The Action Step

Salespeople must know where they want to take the customer with their presentation. Because the entire presentation is built upon this premise, salespeople must identify this critical objective.

POINTS TO PONDER — SOMETHING TO THINK ABOUT

1. How much preparation do you actually undertake prior to each sales presentation?
2. What is your typical presentation focus: what *you* want to present or what the *prospect* wants to hear?

TRAINING ACTIVITY — APPLICATION & ACTION PLAN

Think of the viewpoint or perspective of one or more prospects or customers you are currently working with.

1. Based on what you perceive to be their viewpoint, develop answers to the following:
    a. Identify what is important to them.
    b. Determine how they view your product or service or one similar to it.
    c. Establish how important your product or service is to their business.
    d. Uncover the specific issues that spark their individual interest.
2. Compare and contrast your initial perception of their viewpoint against what is actually important to them.

2

The Sales Proposal

The sales proposal forms the basis of most sales and is the foundation of an effective sales presentation. A widely misused, misunderstood and underappreciated tool, salespeople know they must present proposals, but often fail to invest the time and energy in creating them.

IMPLICATIONS — WHAT THIS MEANS TO YOU

While the sales proposal is the workhorse for many salespeople and presentations, most fail to understand the power that it holds. In many selling environments, salespeople will deliver a visual presentation of the sales proposal and then leave it behind for the prospect or customer's further consideration. While many salespeople will mentally link these two, the sales proposal must be considered as a standalone sales tool.

It is important for salespeople to understand that in the typical selling environment, the sales proposal can and will be reviewed by people who were not present at the sales presentation. A poorly written or prepared sales presentation will not adequately convince the prospect or customer and will in many cases undermine salespeople's efforts.

STRATEGIES, TIPS & TECHNIQUES TO APPLY

Many sales proposals are created from the salesperson's perspective. They present products and solutions that they want to sell, but fail to address what the prospect or customer wants to buy. Several key points to remember in developing effective sales presentations include:

Identify the Problem

When salespeople create their proposals, they must understand that the prospect or customer does not want to buy a product or service nearly as much as they want to find a solution and fill a need.

Before salespeople can create an effective proposal, they must clearly identify and understand the prospect's problem, concern or need. Without this critical information, they are building a proposal without a firm foundation for their sales arguments.

Craft a Solution

Salespeople should focus their sales proposal on effectively positioning themselves as the best possible option available to the prospect or customer, thus blocking and ultimately defeating the competition. Salespeople must not only understand the customer's problem or need, but also how the competition will react with their own solution. This is done throughout the entire sales process, but culminates in a strong sales proposal.

Present the Solution

Most salespeople invest the time and effort in successfully identifying the customer's problems and needs and crafting a solid solution, but many fail to effectively communicate it—either verbally or in written form. Some key points for salespeople to remember are:

> *The Prospect's or Customer's Perspective* – One of the most common pitfalls salespeople fall into when developing proposals and presentations is to view and present data and information from their own

perspective. In most cases, unless salespeople are recognized experts in their field, the prospect or customer will not care what salespeople think. They are seeking answers and solutions to problems and pressing concerns.

When preparing a sales proposal, salespeople must think in terms of the customer's interest. When salespeople view the process from the prospect's or customer's perspective, a number of issues will arise that can be adequately answered. These are concerns that would not have been considered otherwise.

What They Need to Know – Another tendency of salespeople is to provide their prospect and customers with entirely too much information. Most feel it is better to err on the safe side and offer too much rather than too little information. It is often difficult to resist including glossy marketing materials and brochures, even if they add little value to the proposal.

Salespeople should consider what the customer needs to know to make a qualified buying decision. When the data and information focuses upon and supports that decision, salespeople should be able to present exactly what the customer needs.

Respect the Customer's Time – In addition to providing the customer information targeted to their needs, salespeople must respect their time. Large and unwieldy proposals—especially when customers are considering multiple proposals from several competitors—will not be read thoroughly. It is better for salespeople to have a crisp, concise proposal, with any secondary information included in an addendum. If primary numbers or facts need to be supported, the prospect or customer should be referred to the addendum, rather than being forced to wade through text in the key sections of the proposal.

Be Concise – Sales proposals should be pointed and concise, with a clear progression that builds upon key points and leads the reader to a logical conclusion. The proposal should be easy to read and use, referring the reader to supporting facts and data in the rear of the proposal. It is far better for salespeople to be brief in their verbal and written presentation than to be longwinded and verbose. Salespeople should make their points quickly to maintain the prospect or customer's attention. A well-developed sales proposal should resemble an extended executive summary. If the prospect or customer needs to see more facts, they can easily refer to the addendum.

Professionally Packaged – With the ready availability of desktop publishing software, it is easy to overdo the multimedia aspect of the presentation and proposal. Each should be professionally prepared and presented. In keeping proposals clean and simple, salespeople should employ the "rule of three," using no more than three fonts, sizes, colors and styles. The final proposal should be neatly printed and bound to create a positive presentation.

POINTS TO PONDER – SOMETHING TO THINK ABOUT

1. How much thought and consideration have you given to the development of your sales proposals?
2. How carefully have you thought about the prospect or customer's informational requirements and time when preparing a sales proposal?

TRAINING ACTIVITY – APPLICATION & ACTION PLAN

Identify the specific information and data your prospect or customer needs to make a qualified buying decision.

1. Create and audit your proposal.
2. Identify the specific information that is essential to keep.
3. Determine the information that should be eliminated.
4. Identify any additional information that should also be included.

3

Problems and Pitfalls of Sales Presentations

While today's technology presents a whole new set of presentation options, the use of laptop computers, digital projectors and PowerPoint presentations can also give salespeople a false sense of security going into a sales presentation. Fancy multimedia presentations are no substitute for a well crafted and compelling sales message. If anything, these presentations can make a poorly crafted sales message appear even more lacking.

IMPLICATIONS — WHAT THIS MEANS TO YOU

The essence of a good sales presentation is a well thought out and properly presented sales message, not a multimedia bonanza. More time should be invested in the message and how well it is communicated than how it is packaged. More often than not, the lion's share of time invested by salespeople is in the media and not the message—a misdirected effort that produces predictable results.

STRATEGIES, TIPS & TECHNIQUES TO APPLY

There are a number of presentation pitfalls that salespeople should be aware of and guard against. These include:

Lack of Knowledge

Many salespeople are guilty of being too tied to their sales proposal and presentation: when they are interrupted or asked a question, they become flustered and are thrown off-track. Rather than smoothly and seamlessly address the question, they appear to fumble for an answer.

During any presentation, salespeople should be extremely knowledgeable about their product, company, customer and competition. Equipped with this knowledge, salespeople should be able to answer any question without a hitch and continue on confidently with their presentation.

Poor Presentation Skills

Salespeople who have difficulty communicating their sales message to their audience display a lack of confidence in their product, their company, and themselves. This undermines their ability to sell effectively and results in the audience distrusting them and their message.

One need not be an expert communicator to successfully convey their message: with enough preparation, practice and rehearsal, anyone can deliver a sales message with polish and confidence.

Lack of Flexibility

Some salespeople are so inflexible that if they are interrupted during the presentation or make a mistake they feel compelled to start over or become so flustered that they lose their place and are unable to recover. This completely destroys the audience's confidence in the presentation and the credibility of the salesperson.

Salespeople should anticipate and be prepared for questions and interruptions. Questions and discussions can be used to provide insight and feedback and gauge the audience's interest.

Poorly Focused Sales Message

Sales presentations need to be designed from the end backward. Each presentation should be focused on moving the audience forward to a commitment stage. The entire presentation should be built upon this and direct and support all arguments that lead the audience forward.

Too Much Reliance on Technology

It is becoming more common for salespeople to use the hardware and software power available to them to create multimedia extravaganzas to impress their audience. However, the sales message is often lost in overdone effects. The audience is impressed and entertained—but not educated and informed, and certainly not moved to make a commitment to the next level.

Technological Meltdown

As salespeople become increasingly reliant on technological gadgetry, many are unprepared for a "meltdown": during the sales presentation, the computer crashes or the projector bulb burns out, significantly increasing anxiety levels during an already stressful event. Emotional reactions can alienate an audience and destroy a salesperson's credibility.

Salespeople need to be prepared for any eventuality and be able to continue the presentation with their sales skills and prepared handouts if necessary. By demonstrating "grace under fire" and recovering from any problems and events that might occur during a presentation they will quickly earn the respect of their audience.

POINTS TO PONDER — SOMETHING TO THINK ABOUT

1. What has your focus been when developing sales presentations? On the message or the media?
2. How have you handled interruptions, problems and technological breakdowns during your presentations?

TRAINING ACTIVITY — APPLICATION & ACTION PLAN

1. Invest time in creating a focused and compelling sales presentation.
2. Focus on the message itself and ignore the presentation media.
3. Polish and make the presentation clear and concise.
4. Once completed, convert it to a Power Point presentation.
5. Compare this presentation to the type of presentation you have used before and note the differences.

4

Know Your Audience Before You Present

Salespeople should appreciate that all appointments are different and that a "one-size-fits-all" sales presentation will not address and meet the needs of all audiences.

IMPLICATIONS — WHAT THIS MEANS TO YOU

All audiences will have a common ground that binds them together, such as the attainment of like goals or the fact that they work in the same company. But salespeople must understand the makeup, composition and distinctiveness of every audience and address the goals and needs of each individual group.

In all of the variables that must be considered in developing an effective sales presentation, if salespeople forget to consider the makeup of the audience, they risk being unable to hold their attention. Adequate preparation demands that salespeople know the individuals they are presenting to and the reasons why they are in attendance.

STRATEGIES, TIPS & TECHNIQUES TO APPLY

Before salespeople begin to prepare their sales presentation, they should create an audience profile of the group or specific individual to whom they will be presenting. The profile should include the following information:

Size of the Group

Salespeople should know exactly how many people will be present at the presentation, as well as their names and titles.

Age

It is helpful to know the age range of the group. This will affect the style and pace of the presentation as well as the type of information the group will seek.

Gender

Often oblivious to the gender makeup of the group, many salespeople will use masculine metaphors—such as sports—to make their points. If the group is comprised of a mixture of men and women, use of these metaphors may be both inappropriate and meaningless.

Knowledge

Salespeople should be aware of the knowledge level of the group regarding the product or service they are presenting. A group with a low level of knowledge will require more background and introductory information, while a well-informed group may consider this condescending. Salespeople must make sure that they are presenting according to the knowledge level of the group.

Education

The education level of the group will determine the types and degree of hand-outs, how much text versus visuals to use, and the kinds of examples that salespeople will use.

Experience

While many audiences may possess knowledge about a product and application, they may have little or no experience and expertise in its use.

Level

Salespeople should be aware of the "rank" of each member of the audience. This includes knowing who the decision makers—as well as influencers—are within the group.

Job Responsibilities

Salespeople should be cognizant of the job descriptions of the individual members of their audience including the challenges they face and the information they require.

Political Agendas

Where possible, salespeople should understand the internal political dynamics of the audience including how decisions are made, who has the ultimate buying authority, and the agendas of audience members that might affect the sale.

Goals, Expectations and Needs

All sales presentations must be developed around objectives, expectations and needs. Salespeople must address the goals of the group and clearly demonstrate their product's or service's ability to meet their needs.

Included in this area is being aware of the decision maker's "hot buttons" or key areas of interest. When salespeople know and understand these points, they can build their entire sales presentation around them.

POINTS TO PONDER – SOMETHING TO THINK ABOUT

1. What sales presentation surprises have you encountered when you did not know who would be in attendance?
2. How frequently do you research the audience and develop a profile before a presentation?

TRAINING ACTIVITY — APPLICATION & ACTION PLAN

Perform a comparison of past presentation experiences.

1. Identify past presentations where the audience was not properly defined beforehand.
2. Analyze the presentation and any pitfalls and surprises that ensued throughout the presentation.
3. Now think of sales presentations where the audience was identified and known beforehand.
4. Contrast the difference in the two presentations and their outcomes.

5

Effective Presentation Techniques

As sales presentations are most often a "onetime shot" with busy customers and prospects, salespeople should do everything in their power to maximize the results of their efforts.

IMPLICATIONS — WHAT THIS MEANS TO YOU

It is surprising how many salespeople really don't prepare for a presentation, but instead will use a canned sales pitch and "fly by the seat of their pants" before their audience.

It is essential for salespeople to understand that just getting by in any aspect of their sales activities is no longer acceptable. More intense competitive pressure than ever before and the availability of more options and choices places salespeople in the position of having to excel and fight for every piece of business they can get. With more demands on time and less access to prospects and customers, salespeople must view every sales presentation as a onetime chance to shine requiring everything they can do to make the best presentation.

STRATEGIES, TIPS & TECHNIQUES TO APPLY

Successful presentations in which salespeople make a compelling case and connect with the audience include several key elements:

Check Your Equipment

Almost all sales presentations are given using some form of electronic medium—most often laptop computers connected to digital projectors. Before any presentation, salespeople should double-check their equipment and have backup batteries and projection bulbs. Salespeople should not wait until they are almost ready to make their presentation to perform these checks.

Have Hard Copy Backups Ready

As with any other technology, things will and do go wrong, with presentation equipment. Salespeople should always have a backup ready, just in case their system goes down and they are unable to solve the problem. Customers can understand technical difficulties, but they will fault salespeople who fail to prepare for them and cannot continue with their presentation.

Engage the Audience

Salespeople should immediately engage the audience within the first 30 seconds of their presentation. Engaging the audience can mean asking a provocative question or imparting opinions, facts and feelings about the subject salespeople are presenting.

Salespeople should avoid long-winded icebreakers or spending too much time talking about themselves and the agenda. The best approach is to start on time and to impart and share usable knowledge and expertise with passion and confidence.

Don't Just Read Information

Salespeople who drone on or race through PowerPoint slides add nothing to the presentation. They are far better served to just display key words and images and verbally convey information not contained on the slide. It is important to impart information and knowledge that is not displayed. Otherwise, it is more efficient to email the presentation and discuss it over the phone.

Talk About What Interests the Audience

All sales presentations should be built around what interests the audience—not what salespeople want to talk about. This is why creating an audience profile is important. It enables salespeople to craft a presentation that speaks to the audience, sparks and maintains their interest and keeps them engaged in the presentation. The use of customer logos and names of specific presentation attendees displays a personal touch that will engage the audience and make the presentation more memorable to them.

The key is to design the sales presentation from the audience's perspective, imparting the information and answers that they want to know about a product or service and the impact and benefits it will bring to their business.

Welcome Questions and Discussions

Salespeople should not view questions and discussions as threatening or damaging to their presentation. A desire for dialogue demonstrates that the audience is interested. In fact, salespeople should incorporate key questions right into the presentation with subsequent slides supplying well thought out answers.

Watch the Time

Salespeople should be careful to work within time allotments. If they are told they have an hour to state their case, they should be prepared to cut their presentation down to allow for questions or other time pressures that are placed upon the audience.

Work Toward a Logical Conclusion

Salespeople should always lead the audience toward a logical conclusion—namely, to make a commitment to the next step or level of the sale. Without a connection to the next step, the audience is left hanging. Thus the presentation should always end with a clearly defined action step.

POINTS TO PONDER – SOMETHING TO THINK ABOUT

1. How actively do you engage your audience during your sales presentations?
2. Are you passionate or laid back in presenting your topic? What results do you see?

TRAINING ACTIVITY – APPLICATION & ACTION PLAN

Develop a polished, attention-grabbing opening to your sales presentation that quickly engages your audience.

1. Identify the key opening points.
2. Identify one point that will immediately grab the audience's attention and get them engaged in the presentation.
3. Determine how best to present that point, either verbally or visually.
4. Practice your opening until smooth and polished.

6

Getting the Audience Involved

An effective sales presentation goes beyond the mere imparting of information and data. It is a demonstration of the salesperson's knowledge and expertise and their ability to personally present a compelling and convincing sales message that brings the audience to a point of commitment. This means salespeople must use their skills to engage and involve the audience.

IMPLICATIONS — WHAT THIS MEANS TO YOU

The more salespeople can get their audience involved in their sales presentation, the more interested and engaged they will become. The importance of getting the audience involved cannot be overemphasized, as it often leads to commitment, especially when linked with a compelling sales message.

Salespeople must apply their creativity and personal presentation skills to involve their listener(s). This is not to be confused with entertainment: involvement leads to commitment, while entertaining the audience can produce a memorable but not necessarily effective presentation. Both elements can be involved; however, salespeople must not lose sight of the goal of the presentation—to gain the commitment of the audience to take the next step toward the sale.

STRATEGIES, TIPS & TECHNIQUES TO APPLY

A well-prepared presentation should engage the audience and get them actively involved. This both maintains interest and creates a relaxed atmosphere that makes the salesperson's job easier and more effective. Several techniques to accomplish this are:

Preparation

Before salespeople prepare their presentation, they should discuss the requirements of the audience with one or two people and what they expect to hear during the presentation.

Presentations should be crafted and customized based upon salespeople's understanding of the problems, projects and requests shared. They should create a set of slides with objectives, questions and answers specifically for the customer.

Presentation Agenda

At the beginning of the appointment, salespeople should display and discuss the presentation's agenda. They should question the audience as to the key points and information they would like to receive from the presentation. In a small meeting setting, salespeople can go around the room and ask each participant's purpose for attending. Responses can be listed on a flip chart or whiteboard and be referred to during the presentation.

Confirm Interest and Agreement

Throughout the presentation, salespeople should refer back to participants' requirements and monitor progress toward fulfilling those needs. Before moving ahead, salespeople should always ask whether there are additional specifics the audience would like to hear.

Effective Use of Silence

Salespeople should learn to effectively use pauses and periods of silence to encourage questions and discussions.

Reaffirm Product/Service Answers

Salespeople should continually present their product or service as the answer to the audience's problems and concerns. This continual linkage reinforces the salesperson's product or service as the solution the audience needs.

Respond Briefly to Questions

Salespeople need to understand a participant's question, answer it and then stop. Other participants should be allowed to ask follow-up questions to clarify answers. This is a far more effective approach than a long and rambling answer.

Action Items

As key action items arise during a presentation, salespeople should list them on a flip chart or whiteboard. This demonstrates that salespeople have heard and noted the request. When individuals see specific items noted, they will tend to move on to other issues. This keeps the discussion moving. Before the meeting ends, salespeople should either respond to and address each item or indicate the future action they plan to take.

Action Steps

Before the end of the presentation, salespeople should conclude with a recommended series of actions that they want the audience to take. A well-developed presentation will have led the audience to this point, so it is only a matter of salespeople summarizing and then making their recommendations to them. Where possible, a specific date should be assigned to confirm the audience's commitment.

POINTS TO PONDER — SOMETHING TO THINK ABOUT

1. How well do you engage and involve your audience in your sales presentations?
2. What have been your successful experiences when you have involved your audiences?

TRAINING ACTIVITY — APPLICATION & ACTION PLAN

Follow the steps below as you prepare for your next sales presentation:

1. Discuss the presentation's agenda with a minimum of two participants.
2. Identify the expectations of the participants.
3. Detail the specific agenda items the audience expects to be covered.
4. Craft specific question and objection slides with responses.
5. Create customer-specific examples for use during the presentation.

7

Making Presentations Memorable

Too many sales presentations are lost in the clutter. During the course of a month, audiences may sit through multiple presentations. After a while, one begins to look and sound like the other. Nothing is remembered and certainly their impact is lost.

IMPLICATIONS — WHAT THIS MEANS TO YOU

The differences between products are what make each unique. The same is true of sales appointments: if salespeople wish to create memorable presentations, then they must do something that is different. The unexpected is what makes a message memorable. It is within the control of salespeople to achieve this if they choose to be creative and innovative in their approach.

Beyond the traditional sales presentation, there are many ways to communicate a message and tell a story. While it is easy to go overboard and use too many visual effects and tools, a few well-developed and placed effects can go a long way toward making a point and cementing it in the audience's mind.

STRATEGIES, TIPS & TECHNIQUES TO APPLY

Salespeople must be creative and innovative in their presentations to make them memorable. A "stand and deliver" approach is similar to the many other presentations audiences have heard before, so they can be quickly forgotten unless something sparks their interest or gets their attention.

Specific techniques salespeople can employ to make their presentations more memorable include:

Do the Unexpected

Audiences are conditioned to see and hear sales presentations similar to the ones they've heard in the past. Salespeople can be remembered by doing something that the audience does not expect. Not only does this make the presentation memorable, but it also lowers the audience's guard as to what is to be said and presented, making them more receptive to the sales message.

Visual Demonstration

While nothing illustrates a point better than a visual demonstration, the common misconception is that they must be elaborate to be effective and memorable. As long as they make the point, they are effective. In 1994, then Speaker of the House Newt Gingrich used an old electronic tube as a visual representation of the technology the FAA was using in the computer age to direct air traffic. It was a simple yet high-impact way to show how outdated the existing technology was.

Salespeople can use visual demonstrations of the current product or service to show the audience how outdated a product or procedure is compared to the solution they are about to show them. This can be done with the actual object or an effective graphic representation.

Product Demonstration

Where possible, salespeople should provide the audience with the experience of using the product or service they are selling. It is often not sufficient to show the audience. Salespeople should encourage and allow participants to actively use the product.

Product demonstrations stimulate creative thinking and allow participants to imagine the possibilities that the product can offer their company.

Hands on Experience

Salespeople need to get their audiences involved with some form of hands-on experience that makes a point and cements the sales message in the participant's mind. The experience may not be directly related to the product or service being sold, but does make a specific point. Once the point is made, salespeople need to link it directly to their presentation.

Personal Involvement

Any means of personally involving the audience in the sales presentation will make it more memorable. While slides or overheads do appeal to the visual and auditory senses, personal involvement might include further appealing to the senses of touch, smell and taste. The greater the number of participants' senses that are involved in the presentation, the more memorable the presentation will be.

> **POINTS TO PONDER — SOMETHING TO THINK ABOUT**
>
> 1. What have you done to make your sales presentations memorable?
> 2. Have you been afraid to be creative and innovative in your sales presentations?

TRAINING ACTIVITY — APPLICATION & ACTION PLAN

Enhance your sales presentation by considering the following points:

Do the Unexpected

1. Determine what audiences are expecting from you.
2. Identify what you can do that will surprise them.
3. Think of a creative way to present it.

Visual Demonstration

4. Outline the key points you want to make during your presentation.
5. Flag points that can be made visually.
6. Determine the visual tools you can use.

Product Demonstration

7. Determine whether a product demonstration is feasible and can be used during your presentation.

Hands on Experience

8. Think of hands on experiences that can be used to make key points during your presentation.
9. Identify the tools you need for these experiences.

Personal Involvement

10. Identify creative and innovative ways to involve your audience in your presentation.

8

What Steps Should the Audience Take Next?

Sales presentations must be a call to action. Salespeople must view them as a sales tool to communicate and motivate the buyers in the audience to make a commitment. While the presentation presents information to educate the buyer, the primary focus must be to sell, not tell.

IMPLICATIONS – WHAT THIS MEANS TO YOU

Most salespeople are familiar with the saying, "telling isn't selling." Yet, the most common pitfall in regard to sales presentations is just that: focusing too much on the "presentation" during the appointment and not enough on the "sales." When this mistake is made, it is not surprising that many salespeople walk away without a firm commitment to action from the audience.

Most audiences that view sales presentations are neither prepared to buy nor ready to make a commitment. Most are there to gather information. Through the mechanism of the sales presentation it is the responsibility of the salesperson to sell them and motivate them to make an immediate commitment to the next step.

STRATEGIES, TIPS & TECHNIQUES TO APPLY

Intended to be more than a means of transmitting information to the audience, sales presentations are powerful motivational tools when properly focused and developed. Salespeople should employ the following strategies to maximize their presentation's effectiveness:

Singular Focus

Every sales presentation should have a single focus: to educate the audience in the fact that what salespeople have to offer is the best option available to them. This is done by successfully positioning the product or service against the competition with a strong and compelling sales message. Armed with this information, the audience should be motivated to make a commitment to move the sale forward.

Compelling Sales Message

Salespeople must craft a compelling sales message that supports the focus of their presentation. The message should be simple and limited to three or four memorable points that induce the audience to buy.

Target Benefits

Salespeople must link the benefits within the presentation to the "hot-button issues" identified ahead of time. This linkage answers the audience's question, "What's in it for me?"

Salespeople who present without knowledge of what is important to the audience are "flying blind"—presenting a list of benefits that they hope will spark interest. The pitfall of the blind presentation is that issues might arise that cause problems and objections that hinder the progress of the sale.

Conversely, if salespeople know ahead of time what is important, they can craft a targeted presentation pinpointing the benefits of interest to the audience that motivates them to action.

Logical Case

Sales presentations must make a strong and logical enough argument for the audience to take action. Each phase of the presentation should build upon the other and lead the audience to a logical conclusion. Random, rambling presentations do not make a compelling sales argument and do bore the audience. At the end of the presentation, the audience will fail to see a connection between the presentation and the recommendations.

Create Urgency

Salespeople must create a sense of urgency in the audience to motivate them to take the desired actions. Without strong needs to immediately act upon, audiences will defer decisions and commitments to a later time when the salesperson is not present. If possible, salespeople should sell the audience to make an immediate decision while they are present to address concerns, answer questions and influence the sale.

Ask for Commitment

As surprising as it might seem, another common sales mistake is failing to close upon the conclusion of the presentation by asking for the audience's commitment to the next step. They may ask for questions, but many are afraid to ask the audience for the sale or the desired outcome.

One approach is to include a slide at the end of the presentation that poses the next action step or question directly to the audience. Once the question is displayed, most salespeople find it easier to verbally discuss their recommendations and to ask the audience to commit to the desired outcome.

POINTS TO PONDER — SOMETHING TO THINK ABOUT

1. How often do you *tell* rather than *sell* during your presentations?
2. How do you motivate the audience to take action?

TRAINING ACTIVITY — APPLICATION & ACTION PLAN

Use the following strategies, focus your sales presentation on selling rather than telling your audience:

1. Determine the single focus of your sales presentation.
2. Develop a compelling sales message of no more than three or four main points.
3. Target the specific benefits that are important to your audience.
4. Craft a logical case that leads and motivates the audience to take the desired action(s).
5. Develop arguments that create urgency to act.
6. Create strategies that make it easy to ask for the commitment.

About the Author

Timothy F. Bednarz, Ph.D. is CEO of the American Management Development Group, Inc. For over 20 years he has researched, designed and authored hundreds of learning and development programs used by Fortune 1000 companies.

He is also the author of *Great! What Makes Leaders Great. What They Did, How They Did It and What You Can Learn from It* (2011).

Speaking Availability

Timothy F. Bednarz, Ph.D. is available for speaking engagements for your next meeting or association event. He can be contacted at 800-654-4935 or by e-mail at timothy.bednarz@majorium.com.

Bulk Sales

Bulk sales of this book or any other titles available from Majorium Business Press. Inquiries can be directed to sales@majorium.com, or by phone at 800-6654-4935.

Quick Order Form

Fax orders: 715-342-1118. Send this form.

Telephone orders: Call 800-654-4935 toll-free. Have your credit card ready.

Email orders: sales@majorium.com

Postal orders: Majorium Business Press, 2025 Main Street, Stevens Point, WI 54481, USA.

Please send the following books:

____

____

____

____

Please send more FREE information on:

❑Catalog ❑Speaking/Seminars ❑Mailing Lists ❑Consulting

Name: ____

Address: ____

City: ____________________________ State: _____ Zip: __________

Telephone: ____

Email address: ____

Sales tax: Please add 5.5% for products shipped to Wisconsin addresses.

Shipping by air:

United States: $4.00 for first book and $2.00 for each additional product.

International: $9.00 for first book; $5.00 for each additional product (estimate).

Made in United States
Cleveland, OH
06 November 2026

47678345R10026